The Rise Of A Dreamer

A Dreamer Awakened

Tarun Thakur

Made with ❤ on the BookLeaf Publishing Platform
www.bookleafpub.in
www.bookleafpub.com

Dedication

To the dreamers who never dared to dream,
To the fighters who battled unseen,
To the ones who walked the hardest roads,
With nothing but courage as their only code.
To my family, who taught me strength,
To my friends, who stood at length,
To the nights of hunger, the days of strife,
To the struggle that shaped my life.
To the city that gave me a chance to rise,
To the love that saw beyond my guise,
To the failures that made me strong,
To the journey that still goes on.
This is for the middle-class boy I used to be,
Who once feared dreaming but now flies free.

Preface

Dreams seemed distant for a middle-class boy like me, but life had other plans. From leaving home with just ₹500 to struggling for survival, my journey was built on resilience, friendship, and love. This story is a testament to perseverance—proof that with determination, any dream can become reality.

Acknowledgements

I express my deepest gratitude to my parents and my family for their strength, my friends for their unwavering support, and my love for believing in me. To every struggle that shaped me and every opportunity that lifted me—thank you. This journey was never mine alone; it was ours.

1. A Life Without Dreams

I never dreamed, I never knew,
If dreams came true for folks like me.
A simple life, school and home,
No visions of what I could be.

My father served, a life so strict,
The world outside, a distant land.
No colors bright, no wonders new,
Just books and rules, a fate so planned.

Then fate had plans beyond my sight,
A storm would come, I'd have to fight.
The path unknown, the journey tough,
But deep inside, I'd had enough.

One step ahead, no looking back,
A road of thorns, a sky so black.
But still, I walked with silent screams,
A boy once blind, now chasing dreams.

2. The Ticket to Freedom

A battle fought with home and heart,
They wouldn't let me go apart.
Yet hunger burned, a fire so strong,
I chose the road, though it felt wrong.

A mother's love, a whispered prayer,
Five hundred rupees, my only care.
A bus, a ride, to a place unknown,
A city where I'd stand alone.

No turning back, no second thought,
A final chance, a war well fought.
Three days, one shirt, no sleep at all,
A job at last—my rise, my call.

Relief so pure, a breath so deep,
No riches yet, but peace to keep.
For now, the world was mine to claim,
A nameless boy, yet proud of his name.

3. Nights of Struggle

The nights were long, the fights were real,
A call center job to break the seal.
From dusk to dawn, my voice would sell,
Yet in my heart, a burning spell.

By day I studied, pages torn,
No food to spare, just hope reborn.
My eyes turned red, my body weak,
Yet I pressed on, refused defeat.

A year and more, I walked this path,
Each lesson learned, each test I passed.
And then one day, a chance arose,
A golden door, my fate enclosed.

Fifty stood, but one would win,
A chance to leave where I'd begin.
A coder now, no calls to take,
A dream once lost, now wide awake.

4. Friendship in Hunger

A single friend, a brother true,
Through hunger, pain, and skies so blue.
No riches there, no wealth to show,
But in our hearts, a bond would grow.

A vada pav, split in two,
A single bed, a sky so new.
We walked the streets with aching feet,
Yet never let our hope deplete.

The nights were cold, the pockets bare,
Yet dreams still breathed in open air.
Yet, when needed, with no one to see,
I'd ask my sister to send some money.

And when success would start to bloom,
He stood beside, no hint of gloom.
A friend in war, a light so bright,
Through darkest days, my guiding light.

5. The First Ride

The first taste of success so sweet,
An EMI for freedom's seat.
A scooty small, but pride so wide,
At last, my own, my joy, my ride.

No one knew, no soul was told,
Yet winds embraced, the nights felt bold.
Through city streets, we rode so free,
A gift I gave, from me to me.

Not wealth nor gold, but steps so small,
Yet proof I'd climbed, not let life fall.
Each road we crossed, each path we spun,
A whisper said, "Your war's not done."

Yet in those nights, with laughter true,
We raced ahead, the struggles few.
Not rich, not grand, but dreams did soar,
A life once plain, now wanting more.

6. Love Beyond Money

She saw beyond my worn-out face,
Beyond my past, beyond my place.
Not wealth, nor gold, nor empty show,
But dreams that burned, a heart that glowed.

Her world was tough, yet love was pure,
A bond so strong, yet so unsure.
Seven days, yet years we knew,
Two souls entwined, a love so true.

No grand affairs, no fancy nights,
Yet morning talks and coffee bites.
She held my hand, through thick and thin,
A simple girl, yet love within.

The world still frowned, the whispers spread,
Yet in her arms, my fears had fled.
No wealth to share, no gifts so bright,
Yet love was ours, beneath the light.

7. The Secret We Kept

In shadows deep, in quiet space,
We loved without the world's embrace.
No parents knew, no ties were bound,
Yet love had made its secret sound.

Each day we met, each night we spoke,
Through smiles and tears, through dreams and hope.
No ring, no vow, yet hearts did swear,
To fight, to stand, to always care.

The world might mock, the world might scorn,
Yet love still bloomed where doubts were born.
No riches yet, no castles grand,
Yet love still thrived, still held our hand.

Through whispers soft and silent gaze,
We danced in secret, lost in haze.
A world unknown, a fate unseen,
Yet hearts still burned where love had been.

8. A Test of Fate

The office halls began to speak,
Their words would echo, sharp and bleak.
The teasing smirks, the knowing eyes,
Yet love refused to break its ties.

Through work we fought, through tasks we won,
Yet still, they said, "Your time is done."
A bond so pure, yet stained with doubt,
Would walls now build to keep us out?

But love stood firm, it did not wane,
Through all the loss, through all the pain.
I left my job, but not her side,
For love and dreams must both abide.

A change ahead, a future bright,
With her beside, my guiding light.
No job could end what fate had spun,
Our love remained—our war was won.

9. A Love Unshaken

Through distance wide and time so long,
Our hearts remained so true and strong.
Each night we met, our souls entwined,
No fear, no doubt—just love defined.

Whispers soft and laughter bright,
Carried us through darkest nights.
Faith and trust in words we weave,
For love's deep roots, we do believe.

In every call, in every text,
Through every trial, every test.
We held our ground, we stood so tall,
And proved that love can conquer all.

Two souls apart, yet never lone,
In patience grew a love full-blown.
Distance faded, time it flew,
And brought me always back to you.

10. Dreams Beyond Walls

A home so small, a dream so vast,
Yet nothing holds when love stands fast.
No wealth, no gold, just hands so tight,
A promise made, our future bright.

A house was far, but hope was near,
Through struggle's path, we walked sincere.
I asked my parents, my sister too,
Without their help, what could I do?

With every penny saved in light,
A vision shaped both bold and right.
No castle grand, yet strong with care,
A place where dreams are free to share.

And when at last the walls stood tall,
We knew we'd won against it all.
A cycle once, now wheels do glide,
And home is where our hearts reside.

11. A Father's Test

Her father's words, a wall so high,
A future painted in the sky.
She stood her ground, she held so true,
With courage fierce, our love still grew.

Rejections came, yet still she tried,
Through tears she spoke, her voice defied.
To prove my worth, to show my name,
No riches bought, just love's pure flame.

A moment turned, a change of heart,
When they agreed, a brand-new start.
With hands held tight, we stood so tall,
No longer bound, we'd risked it all.

The final step, the test was passed,
Our love had bloomed, it stood steadfast.
With pride, we walked, both side by side,
As family smiled, no more divide.

12. The Wedding Bells

From whispered dreams to wedding vows,
Through love's long path, we took our bows.
A journey made from hearts so true,
A love we swore, forever new.

The rings were placed, the vows were said,
With joyful eyes, the past was shed.
No battle lost, no love denied,
Together now, as groom and bride.

Through winding roads and shifting tides,
Through every tear, through laughs and sighs.
We stood as one, with hearts so free,
A love now bound, eternally.

As petals fell, and bells did chime,
We walked ahead, through love's sweet time.
Two souls had met, now one we be,
A journey told through destiny.

13. The Gift of Time

No rush, no race, just steps so sure,
Through years we walked, through paths unsure.
A test of love, a test of fate,
And yet we stood, despite the wait.

The time it took, the trials we met,
Were only steps, not full of regret.
For patience held, our love so tight,
And led us both to endless light.

To those who wait, to those who dream,
The road is tough, the end unseen.
Yet time itself can't steal away,
What's built on trust and love's own sway.

Through years we grew, through time we learned,
That love survives where hearts still yearn.
With patience placed in fate's own hands,
Our love was drawn in golden sands.

14. From Roads to Horizons

he journey began on two small wheels,
Through city lights and hidden fields.
The wind would hum, the tires would glide,
And all we had was time to ride.

The roads we traced, the paths unknown,
With every mile, our dreams had grown.
To tell the world, to show and see,
The beauty life had left for free.

And so we thought, why keep inside,
The joy we felt, the love so wide?
With cameras set and hearts so light,
A story told in frames so bright.

The travel called, the vlogs began,
A dream once small, now life's own plan.
From distant shores to mountains tall,
We shared the world, we showed it all.

15. The Roads We Take

Hand in hand, we took our flight,
To Kashmir's peaks, a world so bright.
The winds whispered, the rivers sang,
In new lands, our hearts began to hang.

From Gujarat's warmth to Kerala's shore,
Each journey made us love much more.
Through Amritsar's grace and Goa's tide,
We roamed the lands, side by side.

Travel became our love's own art,
A passion shared, a beating heart.
Beyond the miles, beyond the skies,
We saw the world through eager eyes.

With every step, we learned anew,
That love grows strong in skies so blue.
Not just a journey, not just a view,
But a bond that deepens, tried and true.

16. The Strength Within

Marriage, they say, is a different lane,
With joy and trials, love and pain.
Where patience builds and tempers bend,
And two hearts learn to comprehend.

Adjustments made, some dreams on hold,
Compromise in stories told.
Yet in the struggle, we found grace,
A love more pure, a strong embrace.

Family ties, a life re-formed,
Through every storm, our love transformed.
No easy path, yet side by side,
Through highs and lows, we found our stride.

Every test, a lesson earned,
Every flame, a love unburned.
Through struggles deep and triumphs vast,
Our love stands firm, built to last.

17. A Dream Shared

I dreamed alone, once long ago,
Of roads to take, of paths unknown.
Yet dreams were small, just mine to chase,
Until I found your warm embrace.

Now every dream is tied with you,
Our passions blend, a vision true.
No single goal, no selfish quest,
But journeys shared, we love the best.

Through winding roads and foreign seas,
We chase the world with hearts at ease.
No fear remains, no doubt to bear,
For side by side, we'll go anywhere.

From quiet whispers to the grandest schemes,
Together now, we shape our dreams.
For life is bright when love is bold,
A story shared, worth more than gold

18. Forever Begins

The road ahead is vast and wide,
With endless sights, with time as guide.
The world awaits, so much to see,
And every step, just you and me.

Not just for us, but those we love,
We chase the skies, the stars above.
To make them proud, to stand up tall,
To prove that dreams can conquer all.

Our journey starts, it does not end,
With every place, with every bend.
We walk ahead, no fears, no past,
For what we build is made to last.

Let's see where fate may lead us through,
The oceans vast, the mountains blue.
With hands held tight, our souls ignite,
Forever starts with love so bright.